Little Cat Feet

Small Poems from Stinson Beach

Richard j. Heby

For the families that welcomed me

The fog comes
on little cat feet.

It sits looking
over harbor and city
on silent haunches
and then moves on.

–

"Fog" by Carl Sandburg

Foreword

Readers of English language haiku may recognize that many of these poems share striking similarities to the haiku you might find in Frogpond or Modern Haiku or other popular journals and anthologies.

There are a few reasons I don't call this a book of haiku (though others may do so and I wouldn't mind). Firstly, most amateur readers recognize haiku as a 17-syllable poem, which may be seasonal in theme, formatted in three lines of 5-7-5 syllables. They feel strongly that they know what haiku is and that it matters.

I'll refrain from calling these poems "haiku" partly because I anticipate some uninformed readers may give my book poor reviews. These poems don't follow a 5-7-5 format and that may upset some people.

There's something else. When I went from uninformed to informed as a haiku reader and writer, I learned many rules and technical terms about haiku. While I've incorporated some of these rules, I've ignored others. I fear that informed haiku readers, likewise, may give this book bad reviews because the poems don't all contain a "kigo" (season word), or "kireji" cutting word, or even two distinct images.

So what are these? They're small poems, involving sensations, human interactions, and natural environments. And they're all born from being in Stinson Beach.

Stinson is a small town in Marin County California. I recently experienced the area on a 10-day trip with my family. Marin County is home to a large population of artists, writers, and the like, and it's easy to see why. The place is magical, unreal, somber, but inspiring.

I hope I've represented Stinson Beach, and the people I found there, in a true light with these poems. If not, well I don't anticipate anyone can get that upset with small poems.

–

The clouds exhale
mountains
of oysters

A cold fog
breath of
vodka

Finding the place
where her father died
among the redwoods

No one recalls
the nameless
wildflowers

The scent of Eucalyptus
I make believe
to know

Golden hills
rolling on
the cyclists

Leaning over the asphalt
the trees find the sun

Whether they're seals
or pelicans
I nap

Skipping a flat rock
on a flat beach
the color of dusk

The squawks
of hungry birds
and a dog

Lost in the weeds
calling the name
of your small dog

Finding nothing in the clouds
but mystery

High tide
the fishermen get lost
in prayer

A puff of parliament
and the misty lagoon

The cyclists and the seabirds
in rhythm

Spotting a sand dollar
$3.99

Sometimes we forget the dead.
Seashells are skeletons.

We row
through the channel
where black water beguiles

Thinking of great whites
in the black lagoon

On a broken branch
the gull ponders
the muse

Two shattered bottles
one for each decade
since her father's death

Reverberating
in the ocean's breath
our ancestors

I swallow the whole ocean
in an oyster

The taste of
biking up mount tam,
blue cheese

We find common ground in hot sauce
after politics

The marriage of
fire and air,
leavened bread

Lucky for seals
they have no feet to go numb
in the ocean

You talk the way the sand feels,
hot and cold

How we fail
to organize the driftwood
wabi-sabi

In equilibrium
the driftwood
falls over

Everywhere we go
a sign of man saying,
"this
is a sign of man"

What a pleasure
the mountains appear again
from the grey

Bobbing its head
I give the lone seal
a smile

Humpback whales
surfacing a memory
of tales

Like the sea birds
the surfers find
the ocean's beat

High tide
the seals
get smaller

Low tide
the birds dance for the sun

Finding nothing in the clouds high tide

Sharp turns
and soft waves
dissecting a hangover

Pondering the poison oak
my finger stings

Golden green
the dunes sprout
spikes

Winking
a hippopotamus
in a driftwood log

Following the scent
of everyone, the dogs
roll in the sand

If the earth is
mine and yours
what difference
if I care only for myself?

In every grain of sand
the bones of every living thing

The fear of inadequacy
in his footsteps
a million questions

The quiet of high tide
in her footsteps
she is holding me

Over and over
the ocean swells
in your stomach

I count my breaths
in every grain of sand

The untouched sand
of a thousand feet

Older than the redwoods
ancient ferns

Doing my best
with the last onion

Finding solace in
a vine of grapes

What but its red leaves
singing the sun's song

The smell of firewood
cutting through the mist
so man is
in order

One by one
the seabirds land
in curious rows

When all else fails
the seabirds still
pecking at the sand

Crushing a sand dollar
in my palm
the smallest beach
is Earth

Without intention
the dandelions wait
to bloom

Forgetting how to walk
I count my steps

An empty vessel
of gin
filled with water
and wildflowers

Laughs come easy
on a 3 point scale
of drunkenness
with a bottle of wine
on each table

Pulling my life apart
I push the jenga
bricks
off balance

The golden sand
bares no fog
but a halo

Pines
press the full air
to pop

Spying a humpback
in the boat vessels
offshore
cloudy lenses

Resisting the knowledge
of what goes on in a hot tub
I let it all sink in

A soft city
twinkles blue
in twilight

The city in the sky
forgets itself
into the soft mist

Ironed into twilight
the moon and a spray of cloud

Exhaling the dim
sky, I
fall in

Like the ocean of your temperament
clouded in idealism

Two cars
pull the dark apart
into opposite directions

Just the headlights
two cars stretch the dark between them

The pleasure of deleting someone completely and a fig

Burning wood
the smell of just rain

Reaching behind
the wind carries
my hat

Made in the USA
Middletown, DE
10 March 2023

26512917R00050